For Parents, Grandparents and Friends

Nature Detectives at Home
Copyright © 2020 by Janice Kelley. All rights reserved.
All photo credits: Janice Kelley

Content of this book are selections from the Nature Detectives series of themed programs. Program information can be found at https://naturedetectivesusacom This publication is intended for use by the original buyer. It may not be reproduced, distributed or transmitted in any form or by any means, including photocopying, for other than the original buyer without the prior written permission of the author; and certain other noncommercial uses permitted by copyright law. For permission requests, contact Janice Kelley at outdoorjan@att.net.

Nature Detectives at Home. Janice Kelley -- 1st ed.
ISBN 978-0-9715467-3-8

Nature Detectives At Home

Table of Contents

7 Nature Detectives Discovery Journals

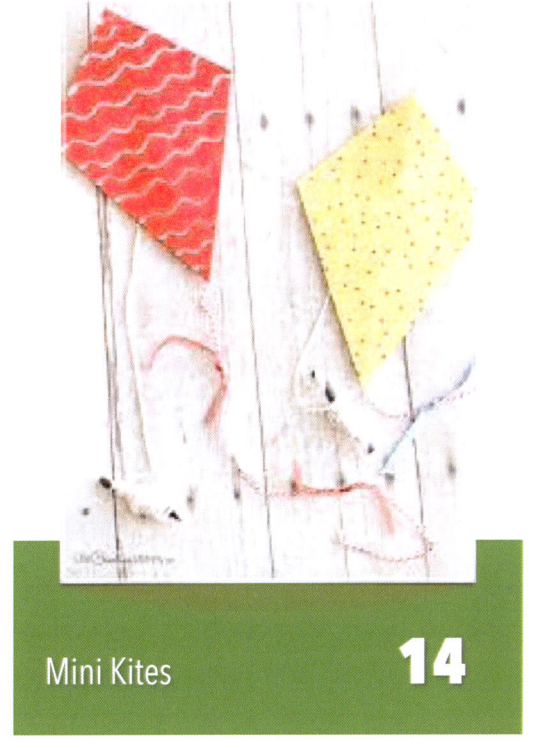

Mini Kites — **14**

9 Observing Leaves and Seeds.

4 **Nature Detectives Bring Curious Minds**
Nature Detectives "teaches fingertips to see." Applying their own curiosity, children take responsibility for their own learning.

5 **Introduction**
List of supplies needed for activities. Where marked, activities are suitable for either younger or older children.

6 **Naturalist Skils**
Lists a set of life skills suitable for any age child or adult.

7 **Nature Journals & Inquiry**
How to get start and questions to pose to increase critical thinking and literacy skills.

8 **Recommended Reading**
Short list of picture books to read and discuss with your child: characters, problems and settings.

9 **Ten Ways to Discover the Outdoor World**
Describes walks, stories and art activities with instructions as needed.

Copyright 2020 - Janice Kelley
All Rights Reserved

Nature Detectives

Where Kids Discover the Outdoor World

At Home
Kindergarten - 3rd grade

Founder and Program Director
Janice Kelley
outdoorjan@att.net

https://naturedetectivesusa.com

Children stay engaged when we follow their Interests and energy.

Step back and watch the magic happen!

Nature Detectives Bring Curious Minds

Nature Detectives activities also contribute to healthy brain development, and improve both physical and mental health. They engage in "Playful Learning" as they run, play, explore, apply hand-eye coordination to measure and count, and practice observation with their eyes, ears and hands. Children feel the texture of tree bark, flowers and soil; closely inspecting them for patterns, insects and fragrance. We refer to some of these experiences as "teaching fingertips to see."

An enthusiastic guide is all children need to create these potentially life changing experiences –
take them outside and encourage them to listen, touch, smell and learn.
A child who is immersed in nature when they are young is far more likely to continue
their connection as adults and be an advocate for preservation of the natural world.

Introduction

This guide presents a sample of *Nature Detectives* activities to enjoy with your children or grandchildren over a period of time. All activities can easily transfer to your home or local park.

Some basic observation activities are suitable for the attention span of preschool age through third grade. *Nature Journaling* and *Citizen Science projects*, can start simple and become increasingly more complex to satisfy interests skills, and attention span of older children.

Tip: Start with one or two simple activities and/or questions to gauge attention span and energy of your child.

Supplies
- Set of 12 or 24 colored pencils and writing pencils
- Blank, white 8 1/2 x11 paper and heavy colored paper or card stock, to create Nature Discovery Journals (can be stapled or 2-hole punched and hand tied with a ribbon)
- Magnifying glass
- Retractable 12 foot tape measure
- 12' plastic or metal ruler

**Additional supplies needed for art activities are listed alongside project instructions.

Looking for a hands on project that is a little more involved and contributes to a database of research at the same time? Listed below is a sample of popular and easily accessible ways to become involved.

Citizen Science Projects

Seek - Mobile app features games to identify photos of animals and plants and learn more about them. Children's version of the **iNaturalist** app..

iNaturalist - Mobile app connected to a worldwide database enabling users to photograph, identify plants and save info using their mobile devices.

Nature's Notebook - USA National Phenology Network
htttps://www.usanpn.org/natures_notebook
Discover and document seasonal changes in plants and animals.

budburst https://budburst.org/
Join the journey to uncover stories of plants and animals affected by human impacts on the environment.

Lost Ladybug Project - Get mobile app on website
http://www.lostladybug.org/
Find, identify and learn about changes in ladybug population.

Naturalist Skills

Activities in this guide are designed to begin building naturalist skills progressively over time.

You can check off what activities you have worked on with your child as a record of their skill development.

Value of Nature Education

The value of children creating meaningful connections to the outdoor world cannot be underestimated. A nature-based education creates numerous opportunities for healthy physical and emotional development, apply problem solving skills, critical thinking and team building.

We cannot expect children to "save the world" when they have not been given opportunities throughout their childhood to love and understand it first.

Find additional activity handouts and scavenger hunts at
https://naturedetectivesusa.com

Naturalist Skills

Safety
- ☐ Water - Stay Hydrated
- ☐ Shelter - Clothing
- ☐ Food - What to eat
- ☐ Awareness of harmful plants & animals
- ☐ Other

Observation
- ☐ Activating all your senses
- ☐ Sitting quietly
- ☐ Using a hand lens
- ☐ Other

Identification
- ☐ Using a Field Guide
- ☐ Animals
- ☐ Plants
- ☐ Rock types
- ☐ Scat/Tracks
- ☐ Weather
- ☐ Other

Mapping
- ☐ Identifying directions (North, East, South, West)
- ☐ Making a Map
- ☐ Reading a Map

Documentation
- ☐ Recording Data
- ☐ Journaling
- ☐ Illustration
- ☐ Other

Measurement
- ☐ Tracks/Scat
- ☐ Trees - Width & Height
- ☐ Water temp & clarity
- ☐ Weather - temperature
- ☐ Other

Nature Journals & Inquiry

Where do I Start?

Nature Journals present unlimited possibilities for children and adults. Some examples below

Write
- Create a poem
- Write key descriptive words
- Record observations or evidence and measurement

Draw (or write)
- A leaf, insect, plant
- Observations
- What is growing in the garden?
- Draw a map (front/backyard or treasure map to follow)
- What insects do you see?
- What color are the leaves? How big are they?

Sensory Questions
- What does the bark feel like?
- What do you hear and what do you feel on your skin?

Sample Basic Journal Questions
Select one, two or three questions to ponder, depending on attention span of the child

Date & Time
I Notice…
Use specific words, pictures and/or numbers

I Wonder…
Who is, was, will it be?
What happened, is happening, or happens next?
Where is, was, will it be?
When did, will it happen?
How does it work?
Why is it this way?

It reminds me of…
Things we have learned seen or felt

Courtesy of John Muir Laws

My Book List

Recommended Reading

A short list of favorite picture books that tell stories of animals and wonders of the natural world. These books present an opportunity to ask your child questions during the story and afterward about the setting, characters, problems they needed to solve and how those problems, solutions or talents may relate to the child.

Animal and art picture books

A Basket Full of White Eggs, Riddle Poems, Brian Swann

Billy's Beetle, Mick Inkpen

Christmas Promise, Lark Carrier

Giraffes Can't Dance, Giles Andreae & Guy Parker-Rees

I Wish I Were a Butterfly, James Howe

The Day the Crayons Quit, Oliver Jeffers

Waiting for Wings . Lois Ehlert

About the Natural World

Discover Nature's Alphabet, Krystina Castella & Brian Boyl

How does the Wind Walk? Nancy White Carlstrom

Water Dance, Thomas Locker

Activity Books

Sharing Nature with Children, Joseph Cornell

Inspired by John Muir, A guide to Studying Nature, Capturing our Stories and Advocating for Wild Places, Janice Kelley

What Song doe the Rain Sing? A Creative Writing and Exploration Journal, Janice Kelley

Find additional resources at:
https://naturedetectivesusa.com

Ten Simple Ways Children Discover the Outdoor World

Search for Clues
Invite your child to bring along their *Nature Discovery Journal* as you walk together. Depending on their age, interest and skill, they have the option to pause and draw what they see on site, or you can take photos for them to either draw from later or attach prints to their journal.

Walk the Alphabet Trail
Read *Discover Nature's Alphabet* as preview of what to look for during your walk through your neighborhood, park or schoolyard. Letters can be found anywhere - fence post, mailbox, palm tree, tree branches, flowers, sidewalk cracks, or sticks on the ground.

Color Walk
Child choose two random colored pencils or crayons. Walk through your neighborhood to find a match for those colors.

Collect, Observe, Draw, Describe
Walking through your neighborhood to find fallen leaves, sticks, pinecones, feathers, seed pods or other natural objects. Take objects home for child to draw, measure and describe. Refer to *Nature Journal and Inquiry* page for question prompts to ask about the object. Invite your child to look for bumps, holes, jagged edges, texture, discoloration, fungus or evidence of insects as they observe.

Look! I see a bird! There is a bird in the tree!

Meet a Tree - *Think of Trees as a Community*
invite your child to "Meet a Tree." Examine the tree with a magnifying glass to get a close up look at the bark, leaves, the base and roots. Look for evidence of insects, spiders, birds, diseases, sap or cuts..

Pose the following questions as they observe to engage their thinking:
- *How do we know the tree is alive? or diseased?*
- *Does the tree look healthy?*
- *Why does this tree grow where it is instead of somewhere else.*
- *How does this tree reproduce itself?*
- *If it has seeds, what are the sizes.*
- *How old do you think it is?*
- *How does it eat - absorb nutrients?*

Ask them to measure the trunk and reachable branches. Assist with measuring their height , waistline and length of their arms.
- Invite comparisons between their body and that of the tree..
- How big is their hand compared to the size of a leaf?
- Where is your child's trunk and branches? What is their bark? How do they get food? How old are they? How old do they think the tree is?

Habitat High Rise
Using your child's journal, ask them to draw what they see at their feet, at their knees, their shoulders and above their head. This activity continues to build their observation and literacy skills ,while focusing on where objects fit in the context of the landscape.

Deep Listening
Ask your child to lay flat on their back on soft ground and close their eyes. Invite them to listen closely to every sound they hear. Ask them to raise their thumb when they hear a sound. Recognize it and ask them to put down their thumb.. Repeat for 2-5 minutes. When they open their eyes and sit up, ask them to identify and describe each sound they can remember: Loud or soft? High or low. Buzz or Whine? If they heard more than one bird or child, how many did they hear?

Sharing Stories

Stories are a lot like treasure chests. The more we dig into the characters, their moods and motives, the setting, and the meaning of the story, the more valuable and memorable stories become. Words on the page are our entry point to the world of imagination and fun. Reading a good story is always better the second or third time. Our first read is a mystery. The next read we learn a little more about the characters and can anticipate what will happen next.

Giraffes Can't Dance and *I Wish I Were a Butterfly*, from the *Recommended Reading* list are both animal stories with many characters to learn about. The deeper meaning of each story is similar – *We all have a special gift or talent to share that others will appreciate*. The main characters believe they are not who they want to be and become very unhappy about it. In the end, each character realizes it has a very special and previously unrecognized talent.

> After reading the story and discussing the behavior of various characters, ask your child, *"What is your special talent?"*

In another story, Billy loses his beetle. As readers, we watch the beetle on each page crawl everywhere in plain sight without being noticed. Invite your child to watch a ladybug, a beetle, a butterfly or a caterpillar. Ask *How does it move from place to place? Where does it go? How long does it stay?* **Nature Detectives** enjoy writing that story in their **Discovery Journals.**

Christmas Promise is a good read anytime. A diverse assortment of wildlife make a home in Amy's tree outside her home. She asks them to promise to leave by Christmas and they do. After all her friends have left her alone on Christmas Eve, Amy makes a wish.

The shortest distance between two people is a story.

A good story can take you anywhere in the world and any place in time.

Nature-Inspired Art

I Love Nature Bookmarks

Instructions
- Use 8 1/2x11 blank or colored paper. Heavier paper or card stock is more durable.
- Child writes or draws a nature "Love Note" on a bookmark and decorates it
    Attaching ribbons, beads or other art supplies is optional.
- One sheet of paper makes four bookmarks.
- Make dotted lines as shown below with a ruler..
- Cut on dotted lines.
- Cut a strip of ribbon about 9" long
- Punch a hole in the top of the bookmark
- Thread the ribbon through the hole and tie the ribbon into a double knot.

Use the bookmark to mark the place in the next nature book you plan to read.

Nature Detectives At Home

Butterfly Fan Puppets

Making butterfly fans is a favorite of many children. These puppets are so they take minutes to make. The popsicle stick or craft post serves as a way for children to carry the butterfly and move it around.

Read, *Waiting for Wings*. This short, large type book features vibrant full color illustrations to display the entire life cycle of a butterfly. End of book features additional illustrations and names of many different species of butterflies.

Supplies

- Colored, white, textured or pre-printed paper - 8 ½ x 11
- 2 pipe cleaners
- 1 ruler or straight edge for straight paper folds
- Colored markers or colored pencils
- 1 popsicle stick or other rounded stick
- Exacto knife or tip of a sharp scissor

Procedure

- Child decorates flat sheet of paper and then folds it into thin sections (about 1") to form a fan. Finish by folding fan in half to form a V. Assist child with folding if needed.
- Wrap 2 pipe cleaners around the center of butterfly body to secure. Each one will become antennae.
- To create hand hold for butterfly puppet, use an Exacto knife or sharp tip of scissor to poke a hole in the center of puppet. Slide the popsicle stick , small round rod or stick from a tree, through the hole.

Mini-Kites

Mini- kites are tiny and meant for light use with light breezes. Use the template and enlarge the pattern. Many *Nature Detectives* created their own patterns to make larger kites.

Mini Kite Supplies

- Kite string
- One or more colors of yarn or ribbon used for kite tails
- Colored construction paper
- Colored markers or colored pencils
- two drinking straws
- Adhesive tape
-

Procedure

- Use template to draw and cut kite shape or modify for larger sizes.
- Decorate.
- Attach drinking straws with lightweight adhesive tape – one strip across the width and one strip taped to the length.
- Attach yarn or ribbon for a tail.

Inquiry-based questions

Aside from the fun collaborative effort to create either a mini-kite or a fuller size model, this is your opportunity to talk about the concept of wind and wind speed. A few questions to ponder with your child.

- What do they feel on their face or in their hair? What do they smell and hear?
- Where does wind come from?
- Do we have wind somewhere in the world all the time?
- What evidence do they notice the wind is blowing?(such as trees swaying)
- What is the effect of wind on our neighborhood n different seasons of the year? (such as falling leaves in Autumn and winter storms).

Mini Kite Template

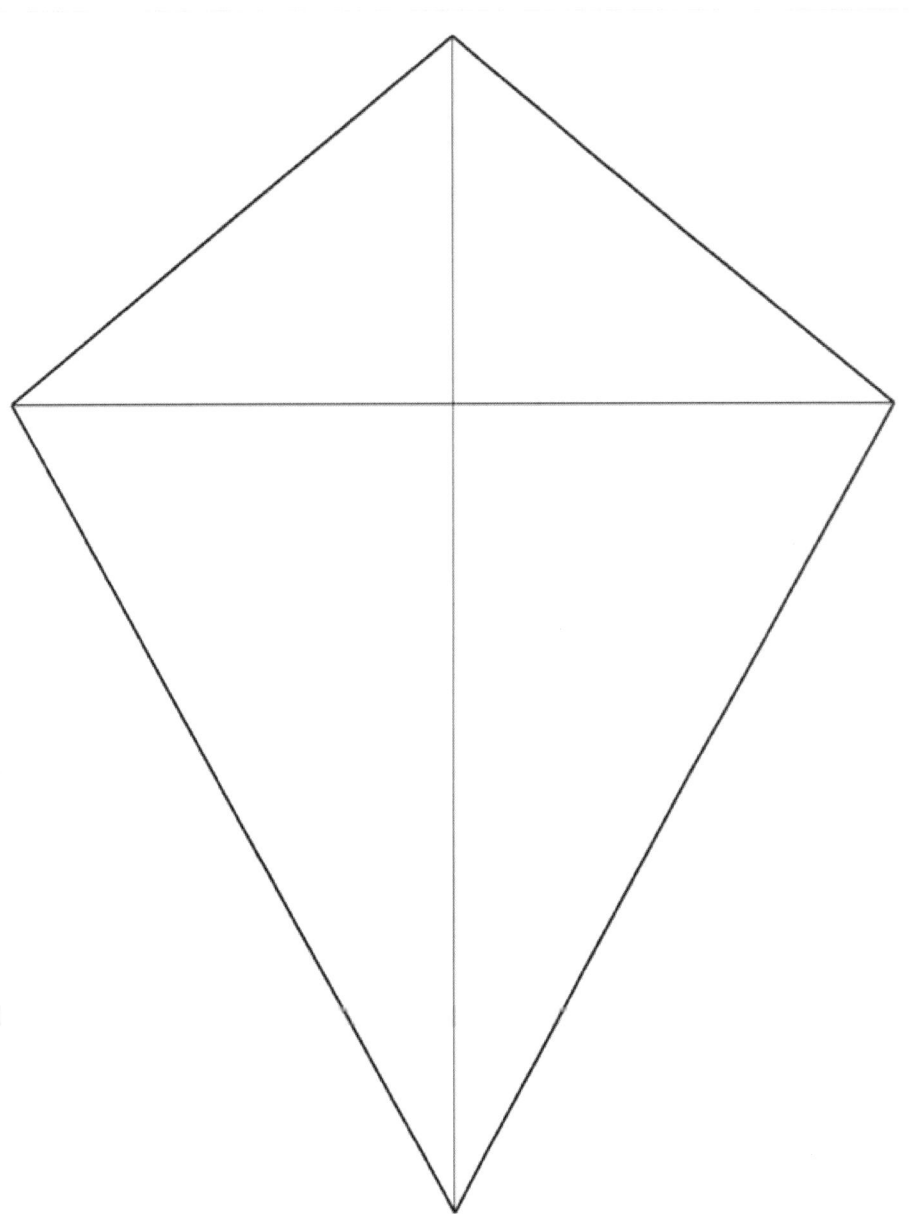

Some children may need you to read the items listed. *Then they will be off and running.*

Nature Detectives love to "find stuff." They won't stop until they have everything checked on their list.

If you can collect some of the items or take a photo, your child has the option to draw a picture in their *Discovery Journal* at a later time.

This activity gives children a sense of accomplishment. The more items they find, the more they want to go out and "find more stuff" to explore.

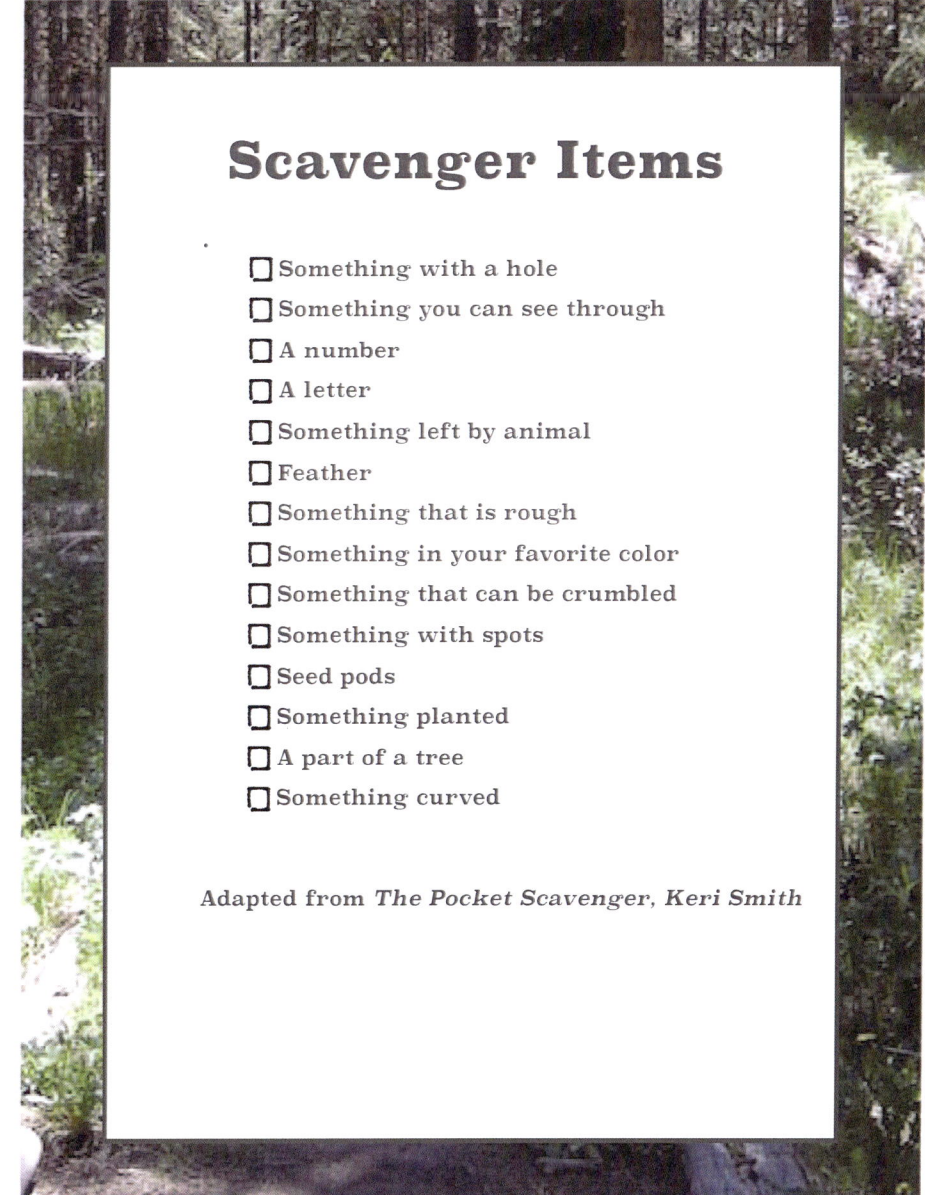

Scavenger Items

- ☐ Something with a hole
- ☐ Something you can see through
- ☐ A number
- ☐ A letter
- ☐ Something left by animal
- ☐ Feather
- ☐ Something that is rough
- ☐ Something in your favorite color
- ☐ Something that can be crumbled
- ☐ Something with spots
- ☐ Seed pods
- ☐ Something planted
- ☐ A part of a tree
- ☐ Something curved

Adapted from *The Pocket Scavenger*, Keri Smith

Create several copies of this **Nature Detectives Passport** *so you can use it over and over again.*

Mark the date & name of activity or activities in each circle, that you and your child do together. For more than one activity per day, insert date on top and list activities on each line

When your child fills up the card, take them out for a special treat - *ice cream is always a favorite.*

Give your children a head start on fostering a good environmental ethic early in life. Visit the website for *Leave no Trace for Every Kid* https://lnt.org/our-work/youth-education/

Nature Detectives
Charter Member

naturedetectivesusa.com

(Card repeated 8 times in a 2×4 grid)

Write your child's name in the blank space underneath the words "Charter Member." Cut apart on solid lines. Place inside a laminated sleeve or pouch and attach to your child's backpack, book bag or luggage. Can also be printed as stickers.

www.ingramcontent.com/pod-product-compliance
Lightning Source LLC
Chambersburg PA
CBRC101937290426
44110CB00010B/189